house beautiful
PAINT

house beautiful
PAINT

The Editors of House Beautiful Magazine

Louis Oliver Gropp, Editor in Chief ❧ Margaret Kennedy, Editor

Text by Rhoda Jaffin Murphy

HEARST BOOKS

NEW YORK

Copyright © 1994 by T HE H EARST C ORPORATION

It is the policy of William Morrow and Company, Inc., and its imprints and affiliates, recognizing the importance of preserving what has been written, to print the books we publish on acid-free paper, and we exert our best efforts to that end.

Library of Congress Cataloging-in-Publication Data

House Beautiful.
House beautiful paint/the editors of House beautiful magazine:
text by Rhoda Jaffin Murphy
p.   cm.
ISBN 0-688-11665-5
1. Interior decoration—United States—History—20th century.
2. Painting—Technique. 3. Decoration and ornament,
Architectural—United States I. House beautiful. II. Title

NK2004.M87 1994   93-42913
747'.94—dc20   CIP

Printed in Hong Kong
First Edition
1 2 3 4 5 6 7 8 9 10

Edited by R ACHEL C ARLEY ❦ Designed by N ANCY S TEINY
Produced by S MALLWOOD & S TEWART , I NC ., N EW Y ORK

Endpapers © Alexa Grace

·CONTENTS·

FOREWORD

*a*s we worked on *House Beautiful Paint*, the newest in volume our *Great Style* series, we realized anew that paint is the most potent decorating tool we have. Whether you want to change the mood of a room, emphasize your own personal style, or add some magic to your surroundings, paint can help. As one designer suggests: Think of paint as makeup.

In this comprehensive book, illustrated with handsome color photographs, we've brought together some of the best ideas our editors have found working with the most talented people in the world of design. We found that a coat of paint can revive a wooden floor, raise a low ceiling, provide a view. And with the magic of tromp l'oeil, paint can even create stone walls, tile a floor, and add paneling or moldings to a room.

In her insightful text, Rhoda Jaffin Murphy explains how creative people use paint to minimize architectural defects, maximize a room's best features, and bring beauty to humble objects. We've included a glossary to help you understand the "language" of paint, along with a reference list of the experts whose work is shown on these pages.

Louis Oliver Gropp
EDITOR IN CHIEF

house beautiful
PAINT

INTRODUCTION

When Boston merchant Peter Faneuil died in 1743, an inventory of his household recorded that one of the bedrooms was painted green, another blue, and a third yellow. That Faneuil could paint his rooms at all is evidence of his affluence. In the Colonies, paint was a luxury that only the wealthy could afford; simple folk used whitewash or left the walls bare.

Fortunately, paint is easier to come by today, but it is perhaps valued even more for its magical ability to bring beauty to the humblest objects and spaces. Indeed, more than any other decorating tool, this versatile and economical medium has come into its own. The simplest and least expensive way to change a room, painting ~ thanks to the enormous range of colors and finishes ~ is also one of the most complex, bringing color, texture, and pattern to every kind of surface.

First and foremost, paint is practical. A fresh coat will instantly revitalize an interior, camouflage cosmetic problems, and minimize architectural defects. Yet, increasingly, homeowners and designers are also taking the decorative potential of paint to new heights; surprising color combinations, innovative floor and ceiling treatments, and special decorative and textural techniques such as marbling, trompe l'oeil, and sponging have never been more popular.

Designed to both inspire and inform, *House Beautiful Paint* explores the limitless possibilities of decorating with paint. In the first four chapters, a portfolio of rooms by designers around the world illustrates how paint can completely change the atmosphere of a room, establish harmony within a decor, create illusion, and accent an interior with personal style. The final chapters offer a practical guide to paint application on walls, trim, floors, ceilings, furniture, and accessories. Finally, an illustrated glossary takes the mystery out of the paint terms most commonly used by designers and other professionals.

Most important, *House Beautiful Paint* invites you to open up your imagination, to conjure up a floor design that no rug could ever match or create a mural that outdoes any wallpaper. However it is used, paint is a rich and valuable design resource that will improve any decor with the most important ingredient of all ~ style.

M O O D S W I N G S

aint is one of the great mood creators. Take a plain white room and put a Chinese red lacquer on the walls, and suddenly the feeling is hot and sassy. But brush a coat of whitewash over rough plaster, and the look becomes coolly elegant; paint a free-flowing mural, and the spirit turns casual and playful. Why such dramatically different effects? Because paint draws on all three of the basic elements of good design ~ color, texture, and pattern ~ and each can be used to set a mood. As a result, paint is one of decorating's most versatile tools. In the two newly built houses profiled at the end of this chapter, for example, one designer evoked a quiet spirit of age with a traditional checkerboard pattern and a palette of muted colors washed with glazes, while another opted for saturated, sunny hues that bring cheerful warmth inside on even the grayest days. In truth, there are no hard and fast rules. The legendary decorator Billy Baldwin advised clients never to choose a paint color simply because it was fashionable, or because a designer recommended it. The best guide has always been personal preference ~ pick the paint treatments you like for your rooms, and they will always make you feel good. ▨

COLOR POWER

The ability of paint to affect the mood of a room most often depends on the power of color ~ to warm, cool, brighten, or darken a space. Much has been written about the psychological effects of color, and different shades definitely do affect people in different ways. Most individuals, for example, find cool colors (greens, blues, and violets) calming, while warm hues (reds, oranges, and yellows) tend to be cheering, even exhilarating. For designers, the traditional rule of thumb has always been to paint rooms with northern or eastern exposures warm colors to counteract the chilliness of the light, and rooms with southern exposures cool colors to mitigate the sun's warmth.

Elsie de Wolfe, the doyenne of American decorating, believed firmly in exploiting the impact of color. When choosing a color scheme, she paid as much attention to a homeowner's personality as she did to the furnishings that were to go into a room. "Nowadays," she wrote in her 1913 book *The House in Good Taste*, "we must consider the effect of color on our nerves, our eyes, our moods, everything." Timeless advice ~ if the interiors here and on the following two pages are any measure. In these striking rooms, color reigns, showing its ability to soothe the spirits and delight the eye.

Any shade in the red family, from the softest petal-pink to the richest rose, is a romantic choice for a dining room. Reds not only set an elegant mood, but also bring a flattering glow to guests' complexions, particularly under candlelight. In this sophisticated dining room, designers Ann Holden and Ann Dupuy relied on the strong wall color and a reflective high-gloss finish ~ rather than an elaborate rug or curtains ~ to establish a glamorous decor and "fill" the space.

Walls the color of summer leaves bring constant serenity to this cool-looking living room. To get exactly the right green, the homeowner enlisted color consultant Donald Kaufman, who uses over-the-counter paint that he mixes himself. Kaufman based the shade on the amount of light the room receives and the color of the trees outside. "We didn't use any green pigment," he says. "We made it entirely out of bright hansa yellow and blue. The yellow supplies warmth and luminosity regardless of shadows."

Cheerful as summer sunshine, a rich, buttery yellow transforms this attic bedroom into an inviting hideaway. Painting the sloping ceiling white helps to "lift" it higher, brightening the space and making the small room feel more airy and open.

A Traditional Look
For a New House

Designer Nancy Braithwaite understands well how to use paint to create a specific mood. In her own Atlanta home she relied on a palette of dusty paint colors, subtly layered and muted with antiquing washes, to impart the mellow spirit of age.

When Braithwaite couldn't find the right old farmhouse for her collection of Early American antiques, she discovered an equally pleasing alternative: a New England–style home built 30 years earlier by Atlanta architect James Means. Although Means's design incorporated several historic architectural features ~ including authentic eighteenth-century paneling, beams, and floorboards ~ Braithwaite felt the pristine appearance of the drywall interiors compromised the overall effect. To achieve a time-worn look, Braithwaite collaborated with Linda Ridings, an artist who grinds pigments and mixes her paints herself.

The design team first plastered the walls, then sanded them to achieve a rough texture. Next came wash over wash of Ridings's own milk-thin casein paint. (Casein, a white protein found in milk prod-

In Nancy Braithwaite's guest bedroom, the antique paneling bears its original eighteenth-century paint. To match it, artist Linda Ridings brushed the window frames and moldings with several layers of gray paint, sanding patches in each. The mottled effect was created by adding semitransparent casein paint over ocher.

ucts, has for centuries been mixed with pigment to make a thin but durable paint.) The walls were resanded, painted yet again, and sanded a final time.

Most commercial paint consists of two pigments, but Braithwaite prefers the depth that Ridings achieves by combining several pigments to create a color. To enhance the natural light in the sun-filled guest room, for example, the designer chose an ocher mixed with raw sienna and a touch of violet to "gray it down and take the sweetness out."

In the master bedroom, a graphic checkerboard pattern strikes a traditional note. After painstakingly laying out the design, the artist painted in alternating squares of linen-white and brown. Veils of taupe-tinted cream and rich butterscotch followed so that no single color would predominate.

These complex applications can take days or weeks to complete, but both Ridings and Braithwaite are perfectionists, willing to experiment endlessly until they have achieved the look they want. "I don't believe in a certain number of coats," says the artist, "I do whatever it takes."

For the master bedroom, the designers chose a checkerboard, a traditional Early American pattern (opposite). More typically used on a floor, the design was enlarged for strong graphic impact on the plaster walls, but quieted with neutral washes so it would look as though it had been in place for years. A dark, saturated hue on the paneling in the same room (left) provides solid contrast and sets off the simple furnishings.

SPARE STYLE AND A PALETTE OF YELLOWS

Yellow, even in its palest shades, is literally a sunny color. Dark rooms instantly brighten when painted yellow; in bright rooms, the warm hue only enhances the light of the sun. Yellow's ability to cheer is clearly apparent in the Hudson River Valley residence of designer Carol Gramm, who used variations of the same base color throughout her new federal-style home. Working with a paint specialist, Gramm tinkered with a custom-mixed Benjamin Moore shade until she got the exact tint she wanted: a subtle ocher with a hint of green. This was then lightened with white or darkened with black, depending on how much sun a particular room receives.

Because the master bedroom gets all-day light, for example, a deep yellow (with more black) worked for this space; conversely, the hallways, which receive virtually no sunlight, are the palest shade ~ a buttery cream that reflects light and makes the space seem brighter and larger.

This convivial family of yellows also provides the perfect backdrop for Gramm's clean and spare interpretation of traditional style. The designer intentionally keeps furniture lines simple and leaves windows unadorned so that the solid wall colors become the strongest elements in all of her rooms.

Yellow evokes a colonial spirit in a new federal-style house designed by New York architect Heather Faulding for Carol Gramm. In the master bedroom, the wall color was chosen to make the most of the natural sunlight while picking up the warm tints inherent in the cherry floor and in the mahogany, oak, maple, and pine country furnishings.

Gramm freely admits that she doesn't believe in clutter or distracting pattern. "I like clean lines," she says. "To get a new look, I simply change the paint and the slipcovers."

Here, simplicity is the rule: as the wall color establishes a definite background, every element in the room takes on special importance. As a result, the furniture pieces themselves become the accessories. And, the decorating lesson becomes pointedly clear: When the color is right, paint is decoration enough.

The inspiration for the base color of the walls came from two sources: the pale yellow hue of the house's exterior and the creamy tints in the designer's collection of yellowware, including the bowl on the bedside table (opposite).

The buttery color is a perfect foil for snowy white bed linens. Setting off the yellow walls, glossy white paint highlights the window trim and the mantel (below), a federal-period piece discovered by Gramm in an Atlanta antiques shop.

CHAPTER **2**

TONES OF HARMONY

t the heart of any successful decor lies harmony. Perhaps Edith Wharton and Ogden Codman, Jr., put it best: "The desire for symmetry, for balance, for rhythm," claimed the influential tastemakers in their 1897 book *The Decoration of Houses*, "is one of the most inveterate of human instincts." One need only consider a much-loved room to know how true this is. In the most pleasing decors, all the disparate elements ~ the architectural details, colors, patterns, and scale and style of the furnishings ~ work imperceptibly in unison. Not surprisingly, a good paint scheme is important for creating this kind of symbiosis. One of the two houses profiled in this chapter shows how paint might become the focal point of an interior, suggesting furnishings that accent the effect but don't compete with it. The second illustrates how paint colors can place a decor firmly in a specific historical period, serving as a more subtle complement to antique furnishings and vintage architectural features. In either case, however, success depends not only on the paint treatment itself, but also on how it relates to the other elements in the room. That relationship, or balance, is the secret to harmony. ▣

PAINT AS A
UNIFYING FORCE

One of the easiest ways to determine the paint scheme for a room is to focus on one element that will trigger the colors. In this living room, designed by Bunny Williams, the raspberry and cream hues of the chintz sofa and chair upholstery were the inspiration for the wall colors. Limited to the paneled dado, the window trim, and the drapery pole, the deep rose paint helps unify the different patterns without overwhelming them.

Designed to create harmony, a paint scheme can work hard: It might establish a theme for a decor, pull together a mélange of apparently unrelated details, or underscore a specific color scheme or fabric pattern.

In its practical function as a unifying design element, in fact, paint does much to take the intimidation out of decorating. Incorporating several different fabric prints in the same room, for example, will seem less risky if you choose a single paint color for the walls or floor that is common to each pattern. Similarly, brushing on the same shade in adjoining rooms is a sure way to make the spaces compatible. If similar but not identical hues are used, a unifying trim color can be the common thread.

In devising a paint scheme, balance within the decor is important. A paint treatment that calls attention to itself ~ a vivid solid color, perhaps, or a whimsical mural ~ tends to work best if it doesn't have to compete too hard with the furnishings in a room. By the same logic, a setting with ornately carved antiques and sumptuous fabrics may call for calmer surroundings. As a general rule, the more eclectic the elements in a room, the more important is the tie that binds them all together.

In a bright and airy
sunroom (opposite), a
trellis floor pattern,
walls the pale blue of a
morning sky, and wain-
scoting painted
picket-fence white help
make sense out of a mix
of indoor and outdoor
furnishings. The stenciled
floor is the room's
anchor: It immediately
sets a garden mood.

The designer, Parker
Saunders, began by
peeling off the old
linoleum to reveal the
original oak flooring.
Next came a coat of fresh
white paint; the trellis
was then painted on top.
   In a handsome
bedroom (above), designed
by J. Hyde Crawford,
a coat of cranberry-red
paint ties together the

strong but very different
patterns found in the
curtains, the needlepoint
rug, and the vintage quilt.
The red color also provides
an elegant backdrop
for a collection of antique
paintings and prints;
because of the greater
contrast, it sets them off
more effectively than
would a simple white
wall surface.

The soft, dreamy paint colors found throughout this 1760 English country house designed by Robert Perkins are undeniably romantic. Yet they also create a tranquil balance between the Gothic detailing and the seventeenth- and eighteenth-century furnishings. A classic English color, Suffolk Pink, was chosen for the first-floor bedroom (above), which gets only morning light. This gentle shade continues to warm the space even when the sun has faded. The same color blends the bedroom with the bathroom (opposite), brightening the room, which has no windows.

CITRUS HUES AND CALMING NEUTRALS

For Mary Douglas Drysdale, a single word defines the most important element in achieving harmony in a room: balance. As if to prove her point, the designer used a surprising range of brilliant citrus paint colors in a very grand Washington, D.C., residence to take traditional style to dazzling new heights. Yet, while it might seem risky, the gutsy choice of colors works well because a judicious balance of furnishings keeps the designer's rooms harmonious.

Intentionally, Drysdale let the walls, draperies, and artwork supply the color, while keeping the floors and most of the furniture coverings pointedly neutral. The rugs, of self-effacing sisal, combine with soothing white upholstery to provide a visual respite from the bold surroundings.

Drysdale's eye-catching paint colors ~ from the tangy lemon of the living room to the zesty lime of the master bedroom ~ also strike a balance because they share the same intensity, or strength. "It's just as important to pick the right blend of colors as it is to pick the colors in the beginning," the designer maintains. "In any room you need tonal harmony; otherwise the space will seem unbalanced."

The right blend, however, doesn't just happen. To get the relationships she wants, Drysdale paints 3-by-3-foot squares on the wall until she finds the best shade. Fabric samples also get tacked up, and both paint and fabric are scrutinized under varying light conditions until the designer has decided on the perfect match.

Drysdale also provides areas of relief in a strong color scheme. For example, the walls in the dining room are a flat ivory detailed with white trim. "Transitions between spaces are important to me," she maintains. "I wanted to pick up the yellow tones but reinterpret them in a softer way."

One final moderating influence: The designer has enhanced the paint colors with texture. The living room walls are actually a yellow base color with apricot, brown, and white hues sponged on top. The bedroom walls were first painted bright green, then dragged with a duller green. "The colors were so strong, I didn't want them to hit you over the head," Drysdale explains.

A strong lime green was chosen for the bedroom so that the contrast of the vibrant walls against the dark mahogany furniture would be shocking but pleasing. Simple but stylish pieces like the candlestand show off their distinctive profiles against the rich color. Designer Mary Douglas Drysdale kept accessories to a minimum so that architectural features also stand out.

Drysdale favors decorative dragging for the subtle texture and pattern it provides to a painted surface. In the bedroom (left and right), the technique involved applying a green base coat to the walls, followed by a subtler green; while the top coat was still wet, a special dragging brush was pulled through it to make a semitransparent pattern of wavy lines. The curtains are of inexpensive buff-colored chintz, stenciled with green and burgundy stripes to create the effect of woven silk.

Bold is beautiful in the living room (left above and below), where Drysdale combined tangy yellow sponge-painted walls and bright orange draperies for a cohesive decor. Paint isn't limited to the walls: Gold stenciling along the cornice and on the border of the sisal rug is a unifying detail, adding a special flourish to the decor.

The dining room (opposite) is purposely more intimate than the other spaces. Here a calming ivory wall color was chosen to encourage guests to focus on each other, rather than call attention away from the table as a full-bodied hue might.

R ESTORING A
L ANDMARK

*In this restored colonial
keeping room, accessories
make an important
contribution to the Early
American atmosphere.
Retaining their old paint,
the eighteenth-century
barrels and firkins (once
used to hold grains such
as barley and wheat)
provide accents of muted
color. The wainscoting
and floor were purposely
left unpainted, appro-
priate to the 1789 house,
which is listed on the
National Register of
Historic Places.
Thomas K. Woodard
and Blanche Greenstein
oversaw the restoration.*

The owners of this 1789 federal-period house, dealers and collectors of Early American antiques, had one very clear goal when they began its restoration: to balance historical accuracy with twentieth-century needs. "We wanted to be able to enjoy the house without being burdened by creating a museum," explains Thomas K. Woodard, who renovated the house with his partner, Blanche Greenstein.

Their success is evident in the harmonious interiors of the landmark, which, slated for demolition, had been dismantled and stored until buyers could be found. Now, carefully preserved architectural features, American antiques, and historic paint colors all meld in an interior that respects the history of the residence yet is also practical and eminently livable.

In this house, paint performs an important role in creating the unifying period atmosphere. A combination of new brushwork and original pigment picks up the eighteenth-century spirit of the house, quietly complementing the hewn beams, worn floors, and country antiques.

For help in devising a paint treatment, the owners turned to Susan Connell, an artist and paint expert. Using chemical analysis and simple scraping techniques, Connell determined the colors the walls and floors had been originally painted in 1789: rich blues and deep reds.

Although new layers of paint had been added over two centuries, it was still possible to preserve the original finish in many of the rooms by working gently down to the first coat. After removing the more recent layers, the artist left the softly distressed surfaces alone; in areas where she did apply new paint she used steel wool, dry brushing, and antiquing glazes to match the old paint.

Preferring the natural patina that comes with age, Connell does not always feel bound by historical accuracy. In the guest bedroom, for example, her analysis indicated that the trim was originally a bright blue. However, the paint had yellowed with age, the blue turning to a soft shade of sea green. It was that green that Connell chose to copy in areas that needed repainting.

Similarly, the original paint on the floor of the front parlor turned out to be a bright red. Here, however, the owners decided to create a faded version of a checkerboard stone floor, rendered in paint. Such "marbled" floors were fairly common in the eighteenth century and ~ more formal than a plain painted floor ~ appropriate for a front parlor, which was usually the "best" room in a colonial house.

To the homeowners, submitting to personal preference was far more important than slavishly adhering to a perfectly accurate restoration. In their minds, such flexibility permits history to suggest, rather than dictate, a paint treatment. The result is a perfect harmony between past and present.

In the dining room (left), new shutters added for privacy were painted the same faded blue as the rest of the trim. To get such a soft shade, artist Susan Connell brushed a coat of chalky white over the blue, then added coats of transparent cream and brown. Connell maintains that such layering yields a more convincing patina of age than would a solid pale color. "I paint brand-new old," says the artist, summing up her technique.

To create the marble-look checkerboard floor in the parlor (opposite), Connell first painted solid squares of gray and cream, then added subtle veining with a feather. A border of natural wood gives the pattern a crisp definition. Touched up by the artist, the old paint on the federal-period mantel (salvaged from another building) inspired the bands of gold added to the cornice trim.

In the guest bedroom of
the 1789 house, the lin-
seed oil used as a binder
in the eighteenth-century
trim paint had dulled,
turning the Prussian blue
color to green. Because
the shade was so pretty,
the trim was simply
touched up and left
alone. Similarly, the
homeowners opted not to
paint the chestnut floor-
boards and ceiling
beams, which are all
original to the house;
their natural colors were
too rich to cover up.

CHAPTER 3

ILLUSIONS OF GRANDEUR

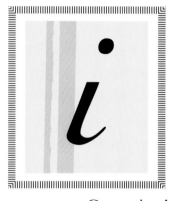

s it or isn't it? That is precisely the conceit behind painted illusion, an artistic tradition with a long and rich history. Both trompe l'oeil (fool-the-eye) painting ~ which relies on shadows and perspective to create an apparently three-dimensional image ~ and "faux," or imitative, finishes date as least as far back as Classical times, when the ancient Greeks painted pottery to resemble marble. Centuries later, "imitation painting," as it was known, became popular in colonial America. Since such desirable materials as mahogany and marble were expensive and often difficult to obtain, woodwork, floors, walls, and furniture were routinely grained or marbled with decorative paint treatments. Painters who specialized in illusion could take the art to skillful extremes. One story has it that when George Washington passed by a portrait by renowned eighteenth-century artist Charles Willson Peale, he bowed politely to two painted figures who appeared to be standing before him on a trompe l'oeil staircase. Such is the power and charm of painted illusion. At its best, it combines wit and artistry to amuse both the fooled and the fooler ~ which is why we still delight in it today. ▨

VISUAL
TRICKS

The ability of paint to create an illusion isn't limited to exotic paint treatments. Paint can also perform numerous practical spatial tricks and can literally cover up problems, such as blemishes and uneven surfaces. In fact, Los Angeles designer Van-Martin Rowe suggests thinking of paint as makeup. "Just as makeup can correct flaws cosmetically," he says, "so can paint correct flaws in a room."

It is possible, for example, to make a long, narrow room seem more in proportion by painting the long walls white and the end walls a warm color, which will appear to advance toward the eye. By the same principle, cool colors seem to recede and tend to make a room look larger. A common method for "raising" low ceilings is to use narrow vertical stripes on the walls. Rowe employs another trick: He often advises clients to paint the walls in a low-ceilinged room a solid color, then continue the same color up onto the ceiling for a foot and a half. As a result, the walls appear to stretch higher, while the ceiling seems to shrink in area and become less dominant.

Paint can also be used to mimic architectural features. A trompe l'oeil column or cornice or a marbled floor can create visual drama, but there are also simpler ways to bring interest to a room;

a stenciled border added to a wall along the ceiling line or where a chair rail might be, for example, will create a sense of scale in the same way as actual moldings do.

It is also important not to overlook the most practical aspect of paint: Nothing serves better to obliterate unsightly or awkward features. A coat of good deck paint, for example, will instantly revive a worn wooden floor. And painting an element you wish to de-emphasize, such as a radiator, the same color as its background will help it to disappear.

A traditional Early American decorative technique, grain-painting was often used on furniture to imitate expensive woods. On a reproduction high chest a soft wash of white adds an updated twist to the effect. On the walls, white paint seems to accentuate the textures of the plaster, and makes the slightest touch of additional color stand out.

*In the serene setting of
this garden gazebo,
painted illusion blurs the
line between indoors and
out. Some 40 years ago,
artist George Oakes
created the moody trompe
l'oeil mural of ghostly
oak trees for the famed
English designer John
Fowler. The effect is
still so successful that
when the present owner,
designer Nicholas
Haslam, rebuilt
the gazebo he left the
painting untouched.*

The dramatic floor in the entrance hall of a traditional home decorated by Mrs. Henry Parish II works double time. The design, painted by Chuck Fischer, not only creates the illusion of striated marble; its exaggerated scale sets an elegant (but not overly serious) tone for the entire house.

This 1950s apartment lacked two things the designer wanted: a proper entryway and an appropriate setting for a dashing George III gilt- *painted console. Gary Crain solved both problems by adding columns in the living room and painting "limestone" walls and a "marble"* *cornice in the refurbished hall. The trompe l'oeil floor is intended to resemble an intricate pattern of stone inlay.*

UPDATED STRIPES IN A QUIRKY COUNTRY HOUSE

Paint and wallpaper have long been in competition for wall space, but the great advantage of paint is its versatility. With a mere lick of the brush, it can be surprisingly easy to create the illusion of a paper wallcovering ~ and often at less expense than the real thing. Moreover, it is possible to enlarge, reduce, embellish, and multiply favorite motifs to suit any space.

It was just that flexibility that was needed to create the decor for a newly built country house in upstate New York, where a collection of quirky nineteenth-century reproductions was intended to be the real star. Serene rather than busy, the paint scheme of this updated Victorian manages to pick up the playfulness of the furniture. In some rooms, rich solids push just beyond the bounds of more traditional color choices. In others, saucy bands of yellow-green and white are stretched as wide as they can go. The oversized pattern (the painted bands are 12 inches wide) avoids the distraction inherent in a smaller stripe, yet appears to "fill" the rooms, making it possible to create a spare setting that requires fewer

Cheerful, exaggerated paint stripes make a playful reference to wallpaper in this New York State country house. To make the colorful bands even, the painters applied a base color, then measured at 12-inch intervals and marked the sections with tape. A final coat of yellow-green in alternating stripes, followed. Old-fashioned moldings combine with the pattern for a Victorian look, reinterpreted for the 1990s.

furnishings and accessories. The painted stripes also show off the eye-catching wicker chairs, spool-turned tables, and scroll-footed stools, providing interest without upstaging the pieces.

In the living room and adjacent sitting room, the green-tinted yellow of the stripes was specifically chosen to offset the French-blue upholstery. Because the blue and green are harmonious (adjacent on the color wheel) they look compatible and help balance one another. Providing contrast, a rich solid blue color appears on the walls of the stair hall, which can be seen from a wide-open doorway in the living room.

The bedroom, in turn, comes alive with a splash of bold sunflower yellow. Here, the woodwork was painted a deeper shade of the same hue to make it "pop." This look is borrowed from the nineteenth century, when popular taste often favored colored woodwork (over white) in a contrasting shade from the walls. But, like the exaggerated bands of yellow-green that appear elsewhere in the house, this fresh approach is very much of the present, maintaining a feeling that is both spirited and young.

To keep the look simple in
the living room, the baseboards, French doors,
and fireplace (top) were
all painted a glossy white,
which purposely echoes the
color of the upholstered
armchair and the coffee
table. The sisal rug also
acts as a neutral foil. For
compatibility, the same
fat wall stripe brings
character to the sitting
room (above).

The French blue on the walls of the entry hall (above) is a lighter version of the color used for the fabric of the blue upholstery in the living and sitting rooms. The stripes in the adjacent space continue below the chair rail so that the extra-wide bands still have a vertical feeling.

The striking yellow-on-yellow color scheme creates a casual air in the bedroom (above), where it makes the traditional furniture appear less formal. Because it is so much darker than the wall color, the strong ocher used to pick out the moldings, trim, and fireplace emphasizes these architectural elements, making them a distinctive decorative force. Such a bold treatment also minimizes the need for extra artwork. When set against this warm background, pieces such as the white wicker dressing table (opposite) are silhouetted clearly, looking clean and fresh.

THE WIT AND WHIMSY OF TROMPE L'OEIL

To be treated to even the smallest glimpse inside the overactive imagination of Richard Lowell Neas is to sense the pure pleasure this artist and designer takes in visual trickery. But for Neas, painted illusion does more than satisfy the impulse to fool; it can also, in a very practical way, bring architectural character to otherwise ordinary spaces.

Neas likes to make a distinction between decorative painting, a visual conceit meant purely for fun, and trompe l'oeil, which is supposed to fool the eye quite literally and make the observer believe he or she is seeing something not actually there. The designer employed both techniques to infuse his eighteenth-century summer home in France with whimsy and personality. The decorative painting in the house ranges from a faux stone tabletop (the playful suggestion of stone) to a trompe l'oeil key hanging from a ribbon on the wall (it looks real).

Neas favors such techniques for the personal touch they bring to a room. "When you paint or have someone paint for you," he says, "it's yours alone." And, as his house illustrates, the conceit is

A visitor to the guest bedroom of artist and designer Richard Lowell Neas may feel a bit like Alice in Wonderland: Nothing is quite what it seems. Trompe l'oeil painting was used to create paneling and a display of faience and delft (left), which copies actual pieces owned by Neas. A striated pattern creates the illusion of marble on the wood top of a chest of drawers (opposite). The fruit is real ~ or is it?

often quite a bit more fun than the real thing.

Visitors always do a double take, for example, after stepping onto the "stone" floor in the dining room, actually created with paint applied over ordinary floorboards. The artist could have used real stone pavers, but, he says, "that would have been the end of it ~ it wouldn't have been anything special." Similarly, in his own bedroom, Neas might have put real paneling on the walls but thought it would be more fun ~ and less costly ~ to paint the moldings instead.

While Neas is a strong proponent of decorative paint techniques, he recommends using these touches as just that ~ touches. Too much whimsy can be overwhelming. "If you do one smashing wall in a room," he declares, "that should be enough."

Neas favors small painterly effects that provoke amused smiles rather than gasps of amazement. In the master bedroom, careful shadow lines produce the effect of three-dimensional moldings and wood paneling.

A trompe l'oeil key (above left) is a sly allusion to the collection of antique keys displayed on the table underneath it. A beribboned portrait and a pair of silhouettes (above right and opposite) are additional whimsical touches.

Food appears never to be in short supply in the kitchen (left), where a trompe l'oeil still life of preserves and fresh produce turns an ordinary refrigerator door into a work of art. To accomplish the look of an old country cupboard, Neas first painted his composition, including the food-laden shelves and the paneled doors, onto canvas, then applied it to the refrigerator front.

In the dining room (opposite), the decoration on a collection of faience inspired the blue-and-white painted decoration on the wooden chandelier. Trompe l'oeil brushwork also transformed the floor with painted stone tiles.

CHAPTER 4

PERSONAL STYLE

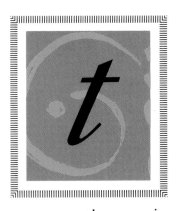

he most appealing rooms aren't necessarily those filled with beautiful objects yet they are almost always spaces that somehow speak of the people who live in them. In essence, they either have, or reflect, personality. While any of the various furnishings in a room can express individuality, the limitless color range and intriguing textures of paint seem naturally to invite the experimentation that makes a decor take off and fly. It isn't necessary to cover every surface; even a small area of color or pattern can alter the appearance of a room dramatically. Brushing a different shade of the same color onto each shelf of a bookcase might be the touch that brings flair to an otherwise ordinary space. Painting the floor a single brilliant hue ~ a surprising red or yellow, perhaps ~ will also make a statement. The exuberant interiors portrayed on the following pages go even further. These idiosyncratic paint treatments illustrate what can happen when a mural splashes onto a wall or ceiling, or when gilding makes borders sparkle with life: Uninhibited and original, these daring interiors are the ultimate expressions of personal style. ▨

FINDING CONFIDENCE

Some time ago, the well-known designer Mario Buatta decorated a client's house from top to bottom. Five years later, he returned and was astounded to find each object exactly where he had left it. When Buatta questioned the homeowner, she explained to him that she had numbered every piece of furniture and each accessory so that she could always return it to the place where Buatta had put it. "It wasn't a home," the designer maintains. "It was a museum."

Buatta's story underlines the fact that confidence in expressing your own personal taste doesn't always come easily. This is especially true with paint: Selecting a bright color or an unusual pattern can be intimidating to even the most assured. But a good designer will always tell a client to follow his or her instincts. The advice is simple: To get a look you really love, look to something you really love for inspiration ~ be it a favorite view, a fabric pattern, or the colors in a bouquet of flowers.

Each of the rooms illustrated here and on the next four pages is successful precisely because the homeowners made decorating decisions based on their own taste, even if they were working with a professional. Taking risks can be rewarding, and the joy of paint is that no mistake is fatal.

For some designers, making a personal statement means juxtaposing the antique with the modern. In the entrance hall of his own Washington, D.C., apartment, designer Gary Lovejoy evoked a look of age by covering the brick walls with thick coats of rough plaster followed by a thin coat of whitewash. The frankly contemporary stair banister creates an arresting contrast.

Los Angeles designer
Thomas Beeton relied on
paint to put a personal
stamp on the interior of
his rented home. In the
foyer (above left), he asked
artist Elloree Findley to
use a strié paint technique
to achieve wavy lines that
echo the structural curves
of the Art Moderne–style
house. Ivory-hued paint
keeps the pattern subtle.
"It's the kind of simplicity
with a twist that I love,"
says Beeton.

In Beeton's master bed-
room (above right), artist
Dana Westring created a
mysterious air by painting
a section of the walls a
bone color, set against
star-spangled persimmon.
A giant urn in the dining
room (opposite) was de-
signed to be a mural, but
Beeton had it done on
paper so he could take it
with him when he moved.
The platinum, gold, and
smoky hues are intended to
be seen by candlelight.

The grandeur of Biedermeier-style furnishings was at odds with a barebones setting (left), until artists from Painted Decoration Studio brushed on architectural elements ~ disguising unsightly baseboard heating in the process. Stenciled gilding provides detail to the cream-colored walls.

Designers from the same group of paint specialists wanted to evince a look of "faded elegance" in a formal dining room (opposite above and below). A coat of stucco was applied to add texture to ordinary drywall surfaces; then came pale stripes of thinned latex in pastel shades inspired by the slipcover fabric. A muddy-hued wash softens the overall effect.

INSPIRATION
FROM A MASTER

For many people, deciding on a paint scheme can be a struggle, but designer Sheila Camera Kotur has a solution: Take inspiration from a well-loved artist. If the color combinations work in a great painting, she reasons, chances are they will work in a room. A favorite composition can also serve as a natural departure point for a personalized design.

When clients asked Kotur to brighten a drab carriage house on Long Island, her own favorite painter, Henri Matisse, instantly came to mind. "When I think of color and the beach, I always think of Matisse," says the designer, who focused on a series of paintings the artist created during the 1920s and 1930s in the South of France. These lush, color-rich still lifes, dazzling landscapes, and sun-drenched views done from Matisse's window in Nice proved the perfect inspiration for a freewheeling design that scampers up walls and onto the floors of the tiny two-room house (the living room and the bedroom each measure 10 by 13 feet).

Abstracting Matisse's borders and signature motifs, Kotur and muralist Sara Nesbitt borrowed the artist's Mediterranean colors, but the composition is their own interpretation. The pair used artist's acrylics for the freehand patterns, while

Dazzling hues inspired by the South of France enliven the living room of a converted carriage house (left and above). "The sun shines so brightly on the Riviera that everything has this vividness," says designer Sheila Camera Kotur. "Anything pastel just seems to fade away."

Benjamin Moore latex paint in over-the-counter colors did the job for the large expanses. The ebullient spirit of Matisse's work made it easy to improvise. No matter that the house had no ocean view; the artist simply brushed a pair of painted windows onto a wall. But the vistas aren't of Long Island: They're of the Côte d'Azur, palm trees and all.

The decor of this pint-sized getaway is the opposite of minimalism. With the painting and the abundant country furnishings, there is a lot to look at. Yet, the designer maintains, such a cheerful space can never be tiring; instead, it is full of "comfort, humor, and atmosphere." Even on a rainy day on the Riviera, the cottage is the happiest place to be.

Kotur made the painted bed coverlet (above) from a length of heavy canvas; a lively border of checks and dots surrounds a pattern inspired by the design on an Aubusson rug. Paint also brings life to the blanket chest and slat-back chair.

More subdued colors appear in the bedroom, permitting the designer to show off the owners' collection of formal portraits and landscapes in elegant gold frames. For extra fun, Kotur threw in what she calls her "bits of surrealism," including a floating bowl of goldfish (opposite). The intricate pillow patterns were painted on canvas.

A surprising plum color was chosen for the floor in the bedroom to sustain the feeling of whimsy. Here, as in the living room, the solution for the old worn scuffed surface was deck paint. The rocking chairs are set to enjoy views of the Côte d'Azur from two imaginary windows ~ only the center window is real.

CHAPTER 5

SURFACE BY SURFACE

orming the backdrop for furniture and accessories, the walls, trim, floor, and ceiling of a room are the basic framework of a decor, and painting any of them sets a scheme around which everything else revolves. The look of one surface in an interior will inevitably alter the look of another, so it is important to consider all. Because it avoids the problems of working out color combinations, a monochromatic paint scheme is the simplest approach. A multicolor scheme, in which the ceiling, for example, might be a different color than the walls and trim, can be more rewarding but perhaps more difficult to devise. Designers recommend the use of analogous colors ~ those that are adjacent on the color wheel ~ because they are naturally harmonious; a blue paint and a green paint with some of the same blue in it, for example, will go well together. Still, a successful paint job does not rely on color choice and decorative effect alone. Using the right paint for the right surface is equally important. Ceiling paint, for example, should never be used on walls because it offers less coverage than good wall paint and can't be washed. Underfoot, a hard-wearing deck paint will last longest.

WALLS

Since walls constitute the largest surface area in a room, they have an enormous impact on the decor. It is easy to be blindsided by the decorative possibilities for these tempting expanses, but visual interest is only one of many factors in a good wall treatment. Indeed, the murals, stenciling, and subtle textural techniques that distinguish the rooms illustrated here succeed because each wall scheme has a purpose ~ to define space, complement distinctive furniture, or perhaps highlight an art collection.

Surprisingly, picking out a solid wall color requires just as much attention ~ maybe more ~ as choosing the subtle shades found in complex layers of stenciling or glazing. A paint chip is usually too small an indicator to be accurate; designers recommend testing as large a swath as possible ~ up to 3 feet square ~ on a wall, and checking it under daytime and nighttime lighting conditions.

Paint finish is another consideration: Three standard types are typically used for walls. Flat produces a soft, matte finish. Eggshell is also soft, but with a slight sheen that is easier to maintain. Satin is the shiniest of the three.

Lighthearted wall patterns will always lift a room's mood, but they can do more: A tiny 6-by-12-foot breakfast room (opposite), was opened up when designer Karyne Johnson made a wall "disappear" with a painted mural of a lushly blooming garden.

"I wanted to invoke the spirit of Carl Larsson," says painter Sara Nesbitt of a whimsical wall treatment (left). A border of yellow garlands adds an important finishing touch to a fresh blue and white paint scheme that calls to mind the work of the Swedish illustrator.

Distinctive furnishings
often call for sophisticated wall treatments that
still remain firmly in the
background. To highlight
a French console and
mirror (opposite), designers Ann Holden and Ann
Dupuy alternated wide
stripes of taupe and
cream, then finished with
a glaze for a muted effect.

Anne-Marie de Ganay
achieved an equally love-
ly effect in an entry
(above right) with a
faux marble wall that
quietly echoes the marble-
topped console.

A subtle wall pattern
(below right) was
devised by design part-
ners Stephen Sills and
James Huniford to set
off a Jean-Michel Frank
armchair and table. The
canvas-covered surface
was glazed, stenciled
with five different pat-
terns in various colors
and tones, then coated
with another layer of
glaze. Thin strips of
painted molding
applied on top suggest
the look of paneling.

The color red brings distinction to an entry designed by Helen Cooper (above). The decorator, inspired by an English manor house, painted the walls in a graphic pattern of oversized diamonds. It shows a traditional Elizabethan color scheme of red and white.

In the hall of a 1731 house (opposite), Thomas Jayne manufactured Gothic mystery with a faux treatment creating the illusion of a wall built solidly from stone blocks. And there is more trickery: Topped with an ogee arch, a wall niche gains dimension from artfully crafted shadows ~ all created with paint.

Painted around 1936, the spare bedroom in the Essex, England, farmhouse of Bloomsbury artists Vanessa Bell and Duncan Grant (opposite) boasts spirited wall patterns inspired by Italian frescoes and the decorated folk pottery of Spain and southern France.

Discovered under layers of newer paint, the cheerful stenciling in designer Sheila Camera Kotur's master bedroom (above right) dates to the eighteenth century. Hand-restoration with watercolors brought the patterns back to life.

Formerly all white, a boxy room (below right) now features walls covered with a Pompeiian red (in latex paint), then stenciled with cabbage roses. A final coating of milky casein paint tempered the colors, so the walls wouldn't look too "new." The designer, Van-Martin Rowe, ran the yellow cornice band onto the ceiling and white baseboard into the floor to "stretch" the wall space.

Conventional wisdom has it that art ~ particularly black and white photographs ~ demands white walls for a backdrop. Architects Paul Aferiat and Peter Stamberg, known for their love of vibrant color, take a different view. When asked to design a bedroom to showcase a collection of Robert Mapplethorpe photographs (below), they decided to do the opposite of the expected and paint each wall a different dazzling color. One is spring-bud green, a second shocking orange, a third bubble-gum pink. The results are far from distracting. "The contrast makes the photographs look much richer," maintains Stamberg, "and it also heightens the sense of surprise."

By contrast, calm colors were chosen for a spacious loft (opposite). Working with designer Mariette Himes Gomez, color consultant Donald Kaufman used a taupe hue to provide a neutral background for the main walls and the ceiling. A medium green defines partitions that create a "box within a box."

TRIM

ainted trim is the finishing touch in a room: White moldings, baseboards, and chair rails will set off a blue room in the same way a white collar and cuffs bring definition to a blue shirt. In fact, whatever the wall color, painting the architectural detailing white always provides a clean, crisp, and classic look. Surprisingly, however, white trim is largely a twentieth-century convention. Common in colonial America, colored woodwork was even more popular in the Victorian era; the 1882 volume *Woman's Handiwork in Modern Homes*, for example, suggested maroon, chocolate brown, orange-green, dark "Antwerp" blue, and even black as ideal trim shades.

A popular approach today is to paint walls one color and the trim a deeper version of the same shade. It can be equally effective, however, to leave the walls white and let the trim provide the color. This works especially well in accenting decorative woodwork, such as an ornate ceiling medallion or an intricate dentil molding. Painting uninteresting woodwork the same color as the wall will help it fade into the background.

Most designers use a semigloss finish, which is scuff-resistant and sponges clean, for trim. The slightly tougher pearl and shiny high-gloss finishes are also favored, particularly for kitchen cabinets.

Interiors with grand architectural features can take on a too-serious tone. In this foyer (opposite and above), walls in a gentle rose fade to white, while glossy trim paint picks up the pilasters, baseboards, moldings, and door frame. The combination is elegant yet understated.

The couple who decorated
this converted horse stable
~ Rodney Ripps, a fine
artist, and Helene Verin,
a designer of shoes and
wallpaper ~ harbors no
fear of color. In fact, the
two thrive on dizzying
combinations, treating
their trim colors with as
much importance as the
walls. In the living room
(left above and below), the
window frames and mul-
lions were painted the
same reddish-purple as
the exterior of the structure
~ shown off by the color of
the front door (opposite) ~
to tie together inside and
out. The warm yellow
wall color was matched to
a manila envelope.

The woodwork of a room
is like a picture frame,
accenting and highlighting
whatever it surrounds.
The owner of this bed-
room (opposite) ~ in the
same house shown on the
previous two pages ~
took the inspiration for
her color scheme from a
classic combination often
used in clothing: red and
navy. Like blue buttons
on a red dress, she says,
the deep blue window
frame and door make a
pleasing contrast to the
beet-colored walls.

   Color contrasts also
define the soaring archi-
tecture of an airy guest
house (right). In order to
draw attention to the
intriguing windows and
to inject needed color,
architects Frances
Halsband and R. M.
Kliment painted the win-
dow trim pale blue-green.
The color emphasizes the
unusual shape and draws
the eye beyond, to the
lush outdoors.

Brilliant lapis-blue trim and white linen walls were used throughout this 1795 New England house to unify a hodge-podge of rooms. The owners, avid collectors of Early American furnish- *ings, chose the blue for the dadoes, windows, and fireplace surrounds because of the color's colonial associations; it was also the perfect com-plement to their prized collection of spongeware.*

The rooms of this historic Massachusetts house, built in 1834, reflect more than a century and a half of changing tastes in interior design. The upstairs sitting room is being restored to the way it looked in the 1930s; the two-tone trim treatment ~ in green and cream ~ on the interior shutters is typical of that period. Because the green is a strong hue, and because the furnishings are rather elaborate, the walls were left a calming white.

Jewel-toned cabinetry and a glittery backsplash not only lend excitement to architect James Hong's kitchen (opposite); the bold colors also help set the area apart from the rest of this wide-open New York City loft. The tall backsplash is made from a burnished steel sheet, sprayed with gold lacquer and coated with clear polyurethane. Spray lacquers for cars, available at automotive stores, provide smooth, clear swaths of blue and purple on the cabinet facings.

A remodeled kitchen (right) was a relic from the 1950s, complete with metal cabinets and stainless steel counters. Designer Peggy Wanamaker revitalized the cabinetry and refrigerator with periwinkle-colored paint, applied with a special heated tool called a hot roller, for a textured finish.

Bland rooms that lack architectural distinction can gain it easily with painted trim. Although the house was built in 1931, this bedroom has a historic air, thanks to painted-on architectural details and several coats of tinted glazes. Designer Bruce Burstert created the look of paneled moldings with a blue-green wash over a base color of watery yellow. Bands of blue also suggest the illusion of a grander ceiling molding, while hand-painted flowers peek over the windows.

Three slightly different shades of Caribbean blue bedeck the interior shutters of a vacation home in the West Indies. Set off against bright white walls, the varying hues echo the colors of the nearby sea and the ever-clear sky. A classic combination for hot climates, the blue and white color scheme always looks cool.

FLOORS AND CEILINGS

Floors and ceilings usually receive less attention than walls but they, too, can be a source of visual delight. A painted floor can offer all the color or pattern of a rug. Even at its simplest, a coat of solid-color paint immediately banishes imperfections in an old or worn surface. A pretty stenciled border, on the other hand, might be used to draw attention to a beautiful wood floor, while a more complex trompe l'oeil design ~ based on the pattern of an actual carpet, perhaps ~ can become a real work of art underfoot.

Painting a ceiling also has a surprising impact in a room. A white ceiling over colored walls, for example, will appear higher than it actually is; a small room with the walls and ceiling the same color tends to feel snug. In an all-white interior, a ceiling painted a vibrant hue will add color and preserve the crisp look. Fast-drying paint in a flat finish is the best choice for a ceiling; glossy paint reveals imperfections, which are typically more prevalent in a ceiling than in walls, showing up as the surface settles over time.

Leading American designer Billy Baldwin often advocated painting ceilings dark, to make them "recede like a clear sky at midnight." In his living room (opposite), used mostly after dark, designer Eric Cohler followed this advice, brushing on artist's oils to bring the night sky indoors and make the room more exciting.

Painter Marilyn Caldwell turned her attention to the floor in a hallway broken up by doors (left). Here, a painted checkerboard helps unify the space and adds drama.

An old wallpaper pattern discovered elsewhere in an eighteenth-century farmhouse inspired designer John Robert Moore to create the floral design for a painted floor (left), which includes a center medallion.

Stenciling with gold powder, artist Linda Ridings painted stars in an unusual octagonal living room (above) to encourage visitors to admire the architectural beauty overhead.

Scandinavian-style rooms are often sparsely furnished yet filled with subtle color. Swedish-born designer Ingrid Goulston used a graphic pattern for a wood floor to introduce design and color to an entrance hall furnished with little more than a painted bench. The daring zigzag design, done in the typically Swedish color combination of apricot and cream, was intended to resemble marble inlay.

This two-story-high, wide-open entry hall demanded definition, but Robert K. Lewis was reluctant to cover the lovely honey-hued wood floors. The designer's solution: stencil a border on the floor to demarcate the space and leave the center area untouched.

Architect and furniture designer James Hong likes sly punches of brilliant hues surrounded by white. He sanded old wood floors (opposite), painted them with two coats of a white epoxy primer, then applied artist's pigments with rags to create a cray-on-box effect. A coat of clear polyurethane pro-tects the design from wear.

In the dining room of a traditional but new house (right), Chuck Fischer painted a floor that mimics stone inlay. The compass rose design reflects the shape of the oval, 14-foot-high domed room and also helps the space seem less imposing by drawing the eye down-ward. The room design is by Mrs. Henry Parish II.

F I N I S H I N G
T O U C H E S

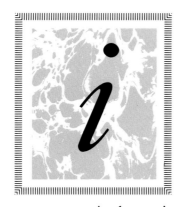

n planning any room, it is all too easy to get caught up in the main elements of the decor: the wall colors, the furniture, the carpets, the upholstery. Yet it is the little touches that give an interior warmth, depth, and richness. Paint lends itself beautifully to detail decorating; it only takes a dab of color to transform humdrum furniture, fabrics, and accessories into something extraordinary. And as painted furnishings become increasingly popular, decorating a piece yourself ~ or enlisting a professional to do the job ~ helps put charming painted items within the range of most budgets. A painted chest or chair will always catch the eye. A hand-painted textile, in turn, is sure to upstage a predictable chintz; even plain white cotton sheets can become beautiful ~ and certainly unusual ~ when detailed with a stenciled border. Painted accessories are another choice. Artfully grouped, they can call attention to a forgotten corner, an interesting piece of furniture, or form an appealing composition in themselves. The great advantage to any painted embellishment is that it makes a room unique ~ and that, in the end, is what lies at the heart of good design. ▨

FURNITURE

aint offers limitless opportunities to add a bit of artistic flair to furniture. Indeed, taking a paint brush to a tabletop or the doors of an armoire can provide the same satisfaction and enjoyment an artist feels when approaching a canvas. Any flat surface naturally seems to invite a pattern or pictorial composition, and picking out small areas with paint ~ the knobs on a drawer, the legs of a stool, or the slats of a ladder-back chair ~ is easy for anybody to try and certain to yield interesting results.

When it comes to furniture, applying a coat of paint is the perfect way to make new out of old. A fresh finish will transform an unattractive piece, disguise rings, nicks, and scratches, and camouflage mismatched materials. Many furniture shops also sell new, unfinished pieces that are ready for the paintbrush.

Vintage pieces are another option. Country auctions and flea markets are excellent sources for reasonably priced furniture that lends itself to a rejuvenating paint job; you may even find usable pieces in your own attic. Old furniture, however, should be inspected for stability and soundness. Paint can cover up surface defects but it can't correct structural problems, such as wobbly legs or poorly aligned drawers.

A free-form leaf border transforms an ordinary glass-topped table (opposite), created for designer Peter Wheeler. Working first on the underside, artist Eric Koek treated the glass with a special pale-green spray paint designed to suggest the look of frosted glass. After outlining the design with a water-soluble pencil on top of the table, he filled in the leaves by hand, using gouache colors. Using paper towels for blotting enhanced the blurry, underwater effect.

Painting a piece of furniture a dark solid color is a good way to emphasize an interesting profile. The deep, glossy black finish on a simple but elegant chair (above) highlights its graceful curves.

While a distinctive armoire (opposite) dates to the eighteenth century, the painting that decorates it only appears to. Inspired by the traditional folk art of the Pennsylvania Germans, the new design was brushed on by a contemporary artist for a homeowner who particularly loves painted surfaces and floral patterns. The finish was then distressed to help make it appear antique.

Although taking a paintbrush to an antique can diminish the value, all may be forgiven if you are a famous painter. Early twentieth-century English artist Vanessa Bell decorated this eighteenth-century French provincial-style bed (above) for her husband, Clive Bell, in 1950. The simple still life is typical of her work.

At architect Byron Bell's weekend home, classic Westport rockers (above) gain a new twist with an eye-catching paint scheme in alternating areas of blue and red. The purple French doors provide a contrasting frame for the lush greenery that surrounds the deck. On the exterior of the doors, the purple at the top fades to blue at the bottom to "echo the evening sky."

Bearing its original paint, an antique armoire from Denmark (opposite) reflects one homeowner's passion for all things blue. On the painted panels and cornice, deep blue veining creates the look of striated marble. The bold piece becomes a focal point in a living room decorated by William Diamond and Anthony Baratta, where white wicker and pale paint colors set an otherwise quiet tone.

New paint can revive fur-
niture that has seen better
days, such as this Regency-
style table (above). While
the piece boasted good
lines and interesting legs,
the top was in consider-
able disrepair. Artist
Richard Lowell Neas gave
it a new lease on life with
a faux marble pattern.

The secret to creating the
cream-colored bands
of "stone inlay" was
masking tape, applied
before the surface was
marbled. When the tape
was lifted, the solid base
color showed through.
    Old paint also has its
own appeal. The original
green and yellow color

scheme of a whimsical
1920s chest (opposite) was
ideal for establishing a
summery mood in a
seaside cottage bedroom.
The slight wear, a sign of
a long and useful life,
only makes the piece
more interesting.

FABRICS

Nothing does more to give ordinary textiles a unique appearance than paint. Stenciling, stamping, and freehand painting on fabric also provide an ideal way to coordinate furnishings with other painted decoration; a valance design, for example, might pick up the same motifs that appear in a wall border.

Filmy gauze, humble muslin, and elegant silk are but a few of the fabrics that can be transformed with paint. In general, the tighter the fabric's weave, the easier it is to decorate, but a loose material like burlap can also be treated; natural cotton and linen hold color especially well. Canvas painted with a decorative design and protected with polyurethane makes a great floor cloth. For a hard-wearing design that can withstand washing, paints made especially for fabric are recommended; these come in a wide range of colors.

A vintage bed becomes even more romantic when it is draped in panels of the sheerest gauze, painted freehand in gold (opposite and above). Decorator Helen Cooper deliberately chose the metallic paint to accent the shiny brass of the head- and footboards. The motifs, including playful scrolls and a design inspired by a nearby wall ornament, are repeated on the fabric pillow covers.

Bacchus must surely smile down from the heavens at artist and designer Lyn Le Grice's dining room, where stenciled grapes and grape vines ~ ancient symbols of feasting ~ prevail. The design, one of the artist's own, repeats on the walls and the canvas window shade, as well as on the damask tablecloth and napkins. The same paints were used for the wall stencils as for the fabrics, which can be washed by hand.

A quiet stenciled border
of flowers and leaves ac-
cents the curved edge of a
fabric window shade,
picked up by sunlight
during the day. The
spray-on stencil paint
favored by Lyn Le Grice
creates a muted effect.

ACCESSORIES
AND ACCENTS

etails are those little touches that finish a room with a flourish. For centuries, paint has been used to do just that: to bring beauty and charm to an everyday object, architectural feature, or the corner of a room.

The Chinese invented lacquer to create elaborate trays, vases, and other accessories. The British perfected the art of painted papier-mâché, and country folk the world over ~ in Scandinavia, Germany, Russia, India, and the Far East ~ have established distinctive handcraft traditions by painting even the simplest household objects, from spoons to bowls, to make them more beautiful.

Today, painted accessories and accents remain an effective and time-honored means for introducing pattern and color into a room. Part of the pleasure of experimenting with these finishing touches is that they need never be serious.

Even the most formal rooms are more welcoming with a bit of painted whimsy. A painted pillow, for example, will always make a splash; the same can be said of a prettily decorated bandbox or floor cloth. And a detail or border brushed on in an unexpected place ~ such as on a windowsill or curtain valance ~ never fails to delight the eye.

Big and bold, polka dots make a surprising touch on a blanket chest (opposite), an antique piece that retains its old paint. The room was designed by Carolyn Guttilla.

In a whimsical living room (above) paint brushed onto a wood cut-out creates a trompe l'oeil window valance, hand decorated by Chuck Fischer; the decor is by Libby Cameron.

Much of the appeal of antique painted furniture derives from a faded warmth that comes with time. That same patina of age also can be easily mimicked. An inexpensive reproduction jelly cupboard ~ purchased new and unfinished ~ gained a vintage look with a trompe l'oeil composition of fairy-tale dragonflies, ribbons, and leaves (opposite), the work of artist Francis Greenwood Dearden.

A new Swedish-style wall cupboard (above) now appears old thanks to a paint technique that involved applying layers of color and sanding each down. A final antiquing glaze completed the "aging" process.

Scraping down and restoring an old painted mantel would have been unthinkable for the owners of a weekend house in Long Island, decorated by Vicente Wolf.

The couple felt that the salvaged mantel lent architectural character to their newly built house and liked its peeling white paint.

Unusual architectural elements often become accents in a room, especially when chosen with the other furnishings in mind. Although the rest of the trim in the formal drawing room of an 1812 house is mushroom-gray and the walls white, the mantel was painted dark green. The reason? To draw out the green in the fabrics and to make the mantel the room's focal point.

Screens are among the most versatile of furnishings; easily constructed and painted, they can function as movable walls. Duncan Grant, one of England's Bloomsbury artists, painted this reversible wooden divider (above) in 1913 for the opening of the Omega Workshops, a group of artists and sculptors involved in decorative work.

On a covered patio in Los Angeles (opposite), designer Lynn von Kersting mounted two panels from a vintage twentieth-century screen ~ blooming with a lush floral composition ~ as wall decoration to enhance the outdoor atmosphere.

ANTIQUING
*A brown antiquing glaze applied over a
green base color suggests the patina of age.*

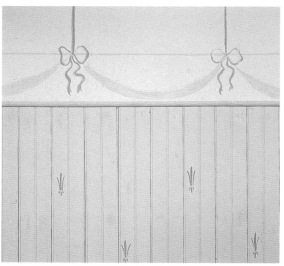

FREEHAND
*Painted freehand, garlands and bows
establish a look of charming individuality.*

GLAZE
*Multiple coats of green glaze create a
translucent effect, subtle shine, and extra color depth.*

GRAIN PAINTING
*Grain painting, here in a checkerboard pattern,
suggests the natural variations in a wood surface.*

PAINT GLOSSARY

ALKYD A durable, long-lasting solvent-thinned paint also known as oil-based paint. Alkyd paint has a strong odor when wet, can take several days to dry, and requires turpentine or mineral spirits for cleanup.

ANTIQUING Also called distressing. A decorative technique for achieving an aged look by applying paint, then sanding it off in patches, or by applying a muddy glaze over a base coat that has dried.

ARTIST'S PIGMENTS Finely ground colored pigments that can be mixed with alkyd or latex paint, or with glazes, to make pure-colored paints.

BASE COLOR The first coat of paint that is applied over the primer.

CASEIN A semitransparent paint made by mixing artist's pigments with casein, a phosphorous-containing protein that is found in milk and milk by-products.

CRACKLING A painting method for achieving a crazed, or cracked, finish by applying two types of varnish over a base color that has dried. As the varnishes react with one another, the crackling occurs.

DISTRESSING See Antiquing.

DRAGGING See Strié.

DRY BRUSHING A decorative technique in which a surface is painted, then brushed with a dry paintbrush while still damp so that the brush marks show.

EGGSHELL A soft matte paint finish with a slight sheen.

FAUX The term for any decorative technique that is used to imitate a particular material, such as marble or wood.

FINISH COAT The final coat of paint used on a surface.

FLAT A slightly porous, matte paint finish.

FREEHAND A technique in which a design is applied by hand, without use of a stencil or a pattern.

GILDING A decorative technique in which liquid gold or gold leaf (real or synthetic) is applied to create ornate decoration, particularly in areas of detail. The term is also used loosely to refer to any metallic paint finish, including those treated to look like pewter, silver, or bronze.

GLAZE A transparent or tinted coating used over a base coat to introduce shine or a hint of color.

GOUACHE COLORS Water-based artist's paints with stronger, clearer colors than standard watercolors.

GRAIN PAINTING A decorative technique in which one or more tools, such as a brush, stick, feather, or fingertip, is dragged through wet paint or glaze to suggest the appearance of wood grain.

HIGH GLOSS A paint finish with a very glossy sheen.

LATEX A water-soluble paint that is generally preferred over alkyd paint because it dries quickly, has little odor, and requires only soap and water for cleanup.

SPONGING

Blue paint sponged over a cream-colored base creates a textured look; heavier dabs provide accents.

STENCILING

Stenciling makes a pretty border for a textured wall surface ragged in blue.

TROMPE L'OEIL

Careful shadowing achieves the illusion of molded paneling in a trompe l'oeil composition.

WASH

A water-thin wash of blue paint enhances the grain in a wood floor.

MARBLING A decorative technique in which paints are blended, mottled, and streaked, often with a feather or sponge, to achieve the appearance of marble. Also called marbleizing.

MILK PAINT A type of paint made from buttermilk and pigments. The term is often used to refer to casein paint.

PEARL A paint finish with a glossy sheen.

PICKLING The painting method for achieving a soft weathered look by applying a flat white paint to a wooden surface, then rubbing some off to reveal the grain.

PRIMER A type of paint used to prepare a surface ~ especially new or unpainted drywall, plaster, or wood ~ so that the finish coat will adhere; also used to cover stains and knotholes and before painting a light color over a dark color.

RAGGING A painting method for achieving a mottled look by applying a base color, then lifting some of the color off by rolling a twisted rag on the surface while the base color is still damp, or by letting the base color dry, then dipping a rag in a second color and rolling it on the surface.

RUBBING A painting method for achieving an aged look by applying a glaze or second paint coat over a base color that has dried, then rubbing it off in a circular motion with a soft cloth while still damp.

SATIN A paint finish with a slight sheen that refects light.

SEMIGLOSS A paint finish with a relatively glossy sheen.

SPONGING A decorative method for achieving a soft, textured effect by using a natural sea sponge to dab one or more paint colors onto a base color that has dried.

STENCILING A paint technique in which color is dabbed, pounced, or sprayed onto a surface through a cutout pattern called a stencil.

STIPPLING A technique in which a special brush, roller, or cloth is used to camouflage brush marks and soften paint colors. Usually, a tinted glaze is applied over a white base coat, then gently treated with the stippling tool to remove traces of the glaze.

STRIÉ Also called dragging. A method for achieving a striated pattern by applying a clear or tinted glaze over a base color that has dried, then pulling a dry dragging brush through the glaze while it is still damp.

TROMPE L'OEIL The term, from the French for "fool the eye," for a flat image that is rendered in paint so that it appears three-dimensional.

VARNISH A hard, clear coating that protects painted surfaces and can also be used to provide a glossy finish. Polyurethane is the most common type.

WASH A paint that has been thinned to achieve a semitransparent effect when applied over a base color that has dried. Often used to give the appearance of age.

WHITEWASH A thin, inexpensive coating made from lime and water or from glue size, whiting, and water. Produces a soft, white, powdery finish.

DIRECTORY OF DESIGNERS AND PAINT SPECIALISTS

Paul Aferiat
Stamberg Aferiat Architecture
New York, New York

Anthony Baratta
William Diamond Design
New York, New York

David Barrett
Circa David Barrett Ltd.
New York, New York

Thomas Beeton
Thomas M. Beeton, Inc.
Los Angeles, California

Byron Bell
Farrell, Bell & Lennard
New York, New York

Nancy Braithwaite
Nancy Braithwaite Interiors
Atlanta, Georgia

Bruce Burstert
Smith and Burstert
Kansas City, Missouri

Marilyn Caldwell
Stonington, Connecticut

Libby Cameron
Parish-Hadley Associates, Inc.
New York, New York

Anthony Cava
New York, New York

Eric Cohler
Eric D. W. Cohler, Inc.
New York, New York

Susan Connell
The Clayton Store
Southfield, Massachusetts

Helen Cooper
Helen Cooper Associates
London, England

Gary Crain
Gary Crain Associates, Inc.
New York, New York

Francis Greenwood Dearden
Lloyd Harbor, New York

William Diamond
William Diamond Design
New York, New York

Mary Douglas Drysdale
Drysdale Design Associates
Washington, D. C.

Ann Dupuy
Holden & Dupuy
New Orleans, Louisiana

Heather Faulding
Faulding Associates
New York, New York

Elloree Findley
Elloree ~ specialist decoration
La Canada Flintridge, California

Chuck Fischer
Chuck Fischer Studio
New York, New York

Mariette Himes Gomez
Gomez Associates
New York, New York

Ingrid Goulston
Ingrid Interiors
Boston, Massachusetts

Carol Gramm
Gramm Design
Garrison, New York

Carolyn Guttilla
Carolyn Guttilla / Plaza One
Locust Valley, New York

Frances Halsband
Kliment/Halsband Architects
New York, New York

Mark Hampton
Mark Hampton, Inc.
New York, New York

Nicholas Haslam
Nicholas Haslam, Inc.
London, England

Judy Hetzel
Briarcliff Manor, New York

Ann Holden
Holden & Dupuy
New Orleans, Louisiana

James Hong
J. Hong Design
New York, New York

James Huniford
Stephen Sills & Associates
New York, New York

Thomas Jayne
Thomas Jayne Studio
New York, New York

Cynthia Lee Johnson
Cynthia Lee Johnson Design
Villanova, Pennyslvania

Karyne Johnson
Panache Interiors
Darien, Connecticut

Donald Kaufman
Donald Kaufman Color
New York, New York

R. M. Kliment
Kliment/Halsband Architects
New York, New York

Eric Koek
Spectrum Painting
Boston, Massachusetts

Sheila Camera Kotur
New York, New York

Lyn Le Grice
Stencil Design, Ltd.
Penzance, England

Robert K. Lewis
R. K. Lewis Associates
New York, New York

Gary Lovejoy
Gary Lovejoy Associates
Washington, D. C.

John Robert Moore
Newtown, Pennsylvania

Sandy Morgan
Sandy Morgan Interiors
Greenwich, Connecticut

Richard Lowell Neas
Richard Neas Interiors
New York, New York

Sara Nesbitt
Hoboken, New Jersey

Painted Decoration Studio
New York, New York

Mrs. Henry Parish II
Parish-Hadley Associates, Inc.
New York, New York

Linda Ridings
Artimura
Atlanta, Georgia

Van-Martin Rowe
Los Angeles, California

Parker Saunders
Saunders and Walsh, Inc.
New York, New York

Stephen Sills
Stephen Sills and Associates
New York, New York

Robert Raymond Smith
Smith and Burstert
Kansas City, Missouri

Peter Stamberg
Stamberg Aferiat Architecture
New York, New York

Lynn von Kersting
Indigo Seas
Beverly Hills, California

Peggy Wanamaker
Kitchen Design. Peggy Wanamaker
Annapolis, Maryland

Dana Scott Westring
Marshall, Virginia

Peter Wheeler
P. J. Wheeler, Associates
Boston, Massachusetts

Bunny Williams
Bunny Williams, Inc.
New York, New York

Vicente Wolf
Vicente Wolf Associates
New York, New York

The room design on page 1 is by David Barrett; the paint treatment on page 7 is by Anthony Cava; the room design and paint treatment on page 8 are by Judy Hetzel; the room designs on pages 11 and 30 are by Mary Douglas Drysdale; the paint treatment on page 15 is by Gary Lovejoy; the room design on page 16 is by Nancy Braithwaite; the paint treatment on page 70 is by Sheila Camera Kotur and Sara Nesbitt; the room design on page 84 is by Mark Hampton; the paint treatment on page 114 is by Lyn Le Grice; the paint treatment on page 136 is by Robert Raymond Smith and Bruce Burstert (top left); Sara Nesbitt (top right); Bruce Burstert (bottom left); Chuck Fischer, room design by Libby Cameron (bottom right); the paint treatment on page 138 is by Francis Greenwood Dearden (top left); Sandy Morgan (top right); Richard Lowell Neas (bottom left).

PHOTOGRAPHY CREDITS

1	Antoine Bootz	74-75	Tim Street-Porter	113	Lizzie Himmel
2	Jack Winston	76	Kari Haavisto	114	Jan Baldwin
4	Tom McCavera	77	Antoine Bootz	116	Judith Watts
7	Jesse Gerstein	78-82	Jeff McNamara	117	Lizzie Himmel
8	Kari Haavisto	84	Feliciano	118	Thibault Jeanson
11	Antoine Bootz	86	Kari Haavisto	119	Michael Dunne
12	James Cooper	87	Tom McCavera	120	Langdon Clay
15	Gordon Beall	88	Langdon Clay	121	Lizzie Himmel
16	Jack Winston	89	Michael Dunne (top) Brian Whitney (bottom)	122	Edgar de Evia
18	Russell MacMasters			123	Thibault Jeanson
20	Jon Jensen	90	Antoine Bootz	124-125	Jeff McNamara
21	Kari Haavisto	91	Langdon Clay	126-127	Jan Baldwin
22	Jack Winston	92	Michael Dunne	128	Kari Haavisto
24-25	Jack Winston	93	Walter Smalling (top) Tim Street-Porter (bottom)	129	Lizzie Himmel
26	Antoine Bootz			130	Jeff McNamara
28-30	Antoine Bootz	94	Kari Haavisto	131	Tom McCavera
32	Peter Margonelli	95	David Frazier	132	Jeff McNamara
34	Lilo Raymond	96-97	John Vaughan	133	Walter Smalling
35	William P. Steele	98-100	Jeff McNamara	134	Michael Dunne
36-37	Michael Dunne	101	Langdon Clay	135	Jack Winston
38	Antoine Bootz	102	Brian Whitney	136	Peter Margonelli (top left) Tom McCavera (top right) Peter Margonelli (bottom left) Lizzie Himmel (bottom right)
40-43	Antoine Bootz	103	Kari Haavisto		
44	Michael Skott	104	Mikio Sekita		
46-48	Michael Skott	105	Walter Smalling		
50	Antoine Bootz	106	Peter Margonelli		
52	James Cooper	107	Jill Kirchner		
54	Michael Dunne	108	Jacques Dirand		
56	Lizzie Himmel	109	Kit Latham	138	Jeff McNamara (top left) Kari Haavisto (top right) Karen Radkai (bottom left) Tom McCavera (bottom right)
57	Feliciano	110	Kari Haavisto (left) Langdon Clay (right)		
58	Antoine Bootz				
60-63	Antoine Bootz	111	Michael Skott (left) Jeff McNamara (right)		
64-69	Jacques Dirand				
70	Jeff McNamara	112	Mikio Sekita	142	Jeff McNamara
72	Gordon Beall				

ACKNOWLEDGMENTS

House Beautiful would like to acknowledge the following homeowners, museums, and businesses: J. Hyde Crawford (page 35), William Thuiller (pages 36-37), Blanche Greenstein and Thomas K. Woodard, *Thos. K. Woodard American Antiques and Quilts*, New York, New York (pages 44-49), Anne-Marie de Ganay, *Juste Mauve*, Paris, France (page 89), Charleston Farmhouse, East Sussex, England (pages 92, 119, 134), Helene Verin, *Fern. I. Tchur*, Lenox, Massachusetts (pages 98-100), Jerry and Susan Lauren (page 102), the Rotch-Jones-Duff House and Garden Museum, New Bedford, Massachusetts (page 103), Stacey White (page 107), Elke Kasman and Bob Sanger (page 128), Janet and William Howard Adams (page 133).

The photograph on page 95 was taken at the Kips Bay Boys' Club Decorator Show House; pages 96-97, the Marin County Show House; page 105, the National Symphony Show House; pages 124-125, the Royal Oak Foundation; page 138 (top right), the Greenwich Show House.